The History of Guitars

Lisa Chesters and Katie Sharp

Contents

Rigby
A Harcourt Achieve Imprint

www.Rigby.com
1-800-531-5015

M000106366

Guitar Music

What is your favorite type of music? If you tap your toes to the beat on your favorite radio station, you are most likely hearing the sound of a guitar. How could one instrument have such an effect on the people who hear it? Let's learn more about the guitar and find out!

Early Guitars

People have been playing the guitar for thousands of years. Around 4,000 years ago, people in the Middle East played the *chetarah*. Five hundred years later, the Romans played the *pandoura*. The ancient Greeks played the *kithara,* and people in ancient Egypt played the *ud*.

ud

These earliest guitars were made from material such as tortoise shells and wood. The strings were made from sheep parts, called gut. Gut was used because it stretched easily.

The ancient Greeks played a stringed instrument called a *kithara*.

Lute

Around 500 years ago, Europeans began playing an instrument called a *lute.* The *lute* is a stringed instrument shaped like a pear. To play a *lute,* you must pluck or pull one string at a time. To pluck a string, you either use your finger or a piece of plastic.

The *lute* was used to play classical music in the 1500s and is still used today.

A *lute* from Italy is called a *mandolin,* and a *lute* from South America is called a *charango.* The first *charangos* were made from shells of armadillos! Today *charangos* are made from wood.

charango

5

Vihuela

Musicians in Spain also played the *vihuela* around the same time. This instrument looked like today's guitar. The *vihuela* is played by strumming, or running your fingers across the strings. Strumming gives guitar music a loud sound. The sound is very different from plucking in which one sound is heard at a time. Strumming allows a player to play many notes at the same time.

Spanish musicians made the *vihuela* popular throughout the world.

The *vihuela* first came to the Americas when Spanish musicians brought it from Spain. It became popular among the native people of the Americas. The *vihuela* makes beautiful music that people can dance to. Musicians still use *vihuelas* in *mariachi* bands, which play music that is lively, fast, and fun to dance to.

mariachi band

Floor plan of a *Mariachi* Band

trumpet player   *guitarrón* player   guitar player

vihuela player   violin player

trumpet player   singer   violin player

Key: ● guitar players

Modern Guitars

In the 1850s, people wanted an instrument louder than the *lute* and the *vihuela*. A Spanish craftsman helped by making a new instrument bigger and louder. This new instrument was called a Spanish, or classical, guitar.

One way to make the sound of a guitar louder is by using strings made with different materials. One of these materials is **nylon,** which people can make into strings. Nylon strings replaced gut strings on Spanish and classical guitars.

Andrés Segovia was a famous guitar player from Spain who made classical guitar popular in the 20th century.

Guitar makers began using steel strings rather than nylon in the early 1900s. A guitar called an acoustic guitar usually has steel strings. When musicians strum or pluck the steel strings on an acoustic guitar, the strings vibrate and make a louder and clearer sound.

Head

Neck

Both the classical guitar and the acoustic guitar have parts that are similar to the parts of our bodies!

Body

Music and Guitars

The guitar became popular with musicians playing many different kinds of music. It was, and still is, easy to carry and take care of.

As a boy in Brazil, Laurindo Almeida learned to play the piano, but he soon decided that he liked the guitar much more!

This guitar player is using part of a glass bottle to play his guitar.

Blues

Blues music began after the American Civil War. When African Americans began moving to the northern United States from the South, life was difficult for them as they tried to adjust to a new place. The African American singers called the music they made "the blues." This kind of music helped them express their feelings of sadness. Some blues guitarists move glass bottlenecks or metal up and down their guitar strings. This is called a slide guitar. The sound this makes is like the singers' emotional voices.

Jazz

As World War I ended in 1917, Americans wanted more lively music. Jazz music combines blues and orchestra sounds.

Jazz guitarist Joe Pass played as Ella Fitzgerald sang.

José Feliciano is a Puerto Rican guitarist known for his Latin-style jazz songs in English and Spanish.

Some jazz guitarists improvise, or invent, their music as they play. Other jazz guitarists supply the background beats for the rest of the jazz band.

This jazz band used more than one guitar.

Country Music

Beginning in the 1920s and becoming more popular in the 1940s, musicians were singing about their lives in the southwestern United States. They sang about things like jobs and love. Although the music made by the guitar is an important part of country music, the words of the songs are also very important. Country music, like blues and jazz, is still very popular today.

Woody Guthrie played an acoustic guitar.

Folk

Modern American folk musicians often use the acoustic guitar to tell people stories about life, freedom, or politics. In the 1960s, some folk musicians, who had only played on acoustic guitars, began to experiment more with a new kind of guitar. People who enjoyed folk music did not like this change, but this new guitar was here to stay.

Joan Baez has been singing and playing her guitar for over 35 years.

The Electric Guitar

This new guitar was called the electric guitar. Even though the acoustic guitar was popular, musicians wanted a guitar that was loud enough for a lot of people to hear. In 1931 the first electric guitar was plugged in. The sound was loud! The guitar and its music would never be the same again.

An electric guitar is plugged into an amplifier, an electrical speaker system that can make a soft sound much louder.

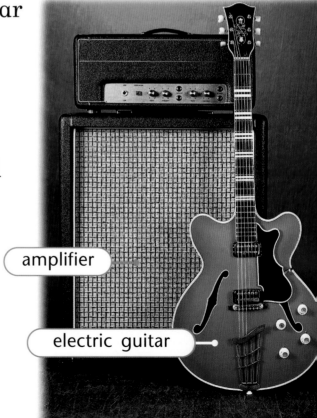

amplifier

electric guitar

Buddy Guy came to play the guitar at a music celebration in Chicago.

Before the electric guitar, musicians had to put microphones near their acoustic guitars to record music and perform for large audiences. The electric guitar has an **electromagnetic pickup,** which is a tool that takes the sound from the vibrating steel strings and sends the sound to the amplifier. Then you are able to hear the music up close and far away.

Ritchie Valens, whose real name was Ricardo Valenzuela, helped make the electric guitar popular in the 1950s.

Electric guitars were made popular in the 1950s. Rock-and-roll musicians played for very large crowds of people. They needed the sound of the instruments to be loud enough to reach everyone. Later some guitarists tried different ways of playing the electric guitar to get different sounds, such as plucking the strings with their teeth.

A lot of music today is made using electric guitars with their loud and upbeat tones. Using electricity to make a guitar louder has changed the way we hear music.

Guitars and Computers

People continue to improve the performance of electric guitars through **technology.** Musicians can now plug their guitar into a computer and try out different sounds. They can also record their music on a computer and then change the sound quality later. Background music for today's musicians can be provided by computer programs. Now almost anyone with an electric guitar and a computer is able to make music!

Did You Know?

- The world's largest electric guitar stands 10 feet 2 inches tall.
- A triple guitar has three necks.

The Music Business

Guitar players began attracting a teenage audience in the 1950s, and they haven't stopped yet. Today guitar players have concerts with thousands of screaming fans. Because electric guitars make loud music, and there are a lot of bands with more than one guitar player, these concerts can be very noisy!

The guitar has changed a lot from the days of the *ud* and the *lute*. And although guitar strings are made from different materials and the guitar has gotten bigger over the years, one thing hasn't changed. We can still hear great music from a guitar!

Electric Guitar Time Line

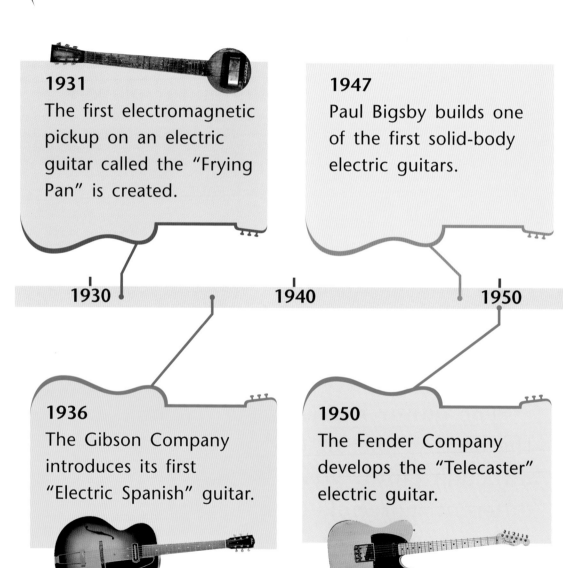

1931
The first electromagnetic pickup on an electric guitar called the "Frying Pan" is created.

1947
Paul Bigsby builds one of the first solid-body electric guitars.

1930

1940

1950

1936
The Gibson Company introduces its first "Electric Spanish" guitar.

1950
The Fender Company develops the "Telecaster" electric guitar.

1961
The Gibson Company makes an electric guitar called the "SG."

1972
Steve Klein begins making electric guitars in odd shapes, including "The Bird," which has a bronze metal bird on it.

1960   1970   1980

1968
The Fender Company designs the "Coronado," an electro-acoustic guitar.

1980
Hugh Manson makes a triple-neck electric guitar.

1980
Electric guitars can now be hooked up to computers to get different sounds and effects.

Glossary

electromagnetic pickup a tool that sends the sound from vibrating guitar strings to an amplifier

nylon a material used to make guitar strings

technology a combination of knowledge, materials, and process used in scientific work

Index